SPY COMMUNICATION

ELSIE OLSON

Abdo & Daughters
MIDDLE GRADE NONFICTION

An imprint of Abdo Publishing
abdobooks.com

ABDOBOOKS.COM

Published by Abdo Publishing, a division of ABDO, PO Box 398166, Minneapolis, Minnesota 55439.
Copyright © 2025 by Abdo Consulting Group, Inc. International copyrights reserved in all countries.
No part of this book may be reproduced in any form without written permission from the publisher.
Abdo & Daughters™ is a trademark and logo of Abdo Publishing.

Printed in the United States of America, North Mankato, Minnesota
052024
092024

Design: Kelly Doudna, Mighty Media, Inc.
Production: Mighty Media, Inc.
Editor: Katherine Chu
Cover Photographs: Adobe Stock, Flickr, Wikimedia Commons

Interior Photographs: Adobe Stock, pp. 1, 4–5, 20; AP Images, pp. 15, 22 (top); Clements Library,
    University of Michigan, p. 27; Federal Bureau of Investigation, pp. 45, 46–47, 48 (top right), 61
    (top right); Flickr, pp. 8–9, 21, 23 (top, middle), 43, 50; IWM, p. 23 (bottom); Library of Congress,
    pp. 24–25, 29, 34–35, 44; Mighty Media, Inc., pp. 58, 59; Shutterstock Images, pp. 6–7, 12–13, 16,
    19, 22 (bottom), 33, 55, 56; Wikimedia Commons, pp. 8, 10, 14, 26, 28, 30–31, 32, 36–37, 38, 39, 40,
    42, 48 (top left, bottom), 51, 52–53, 54, 60, 61 (top left, top middle, bottom left, bottom middle,
    bottom right)

Design Elements: Adobe Stock

Library of Congress Control Number: 2023949220

Publisher's Cataloging-in-Publication Data
Names: Olson, Elsie, author.
Title: Spy communication / by Elsie Olson
Description: Minneapolis, Minnesota : Abdo Publishing, 2025 | Series: Spy guide | Includes online
    resources and index.
Identifiers: ISBN 9781098293147 (lib. bdg.) | ISBN 9798384912415 (ebook)
Subjects: LCSH: Cryptography--Juvenile literature. | Ciphers--Juvenile literature. | Official secrets--
    Juvenile literature. | Espionage--Juvenile literature. | Spies--Juvenile literature.
Classification: DDC 327.12--dc23

CONTENTS

US Central Intelligence Agency
(CIA) agent Paul Dillon was one
of Dmitri Polyakov's handlers.
He gave Polyakov a fishing pole
that contained a secret chamber
for hiding information.

CHAPTER 1

THE PERFECT SPY

IT'S A HOT, HUMID DAY IN NEW DELHI, INDIA. A MAN STANDS along the banks of the Yamuna River. A fishing pole is in his hand, and a tackle box sits next to him. A wide-brimmed hat shields his face from the blistering sun.

Peacocks call to one another nearby. The man casts his line and lets the current carry it downstream. To those passing by, nothing could seem more ordinary. But this man isn't just any fisherman. He is Dmitri Polyakov, a high-ranking military intelligence officer for the Union of Soviet Socialist Republics (USSR), or Soviet Union.

As he fishes, Polyakov mutters quietly. The other fishermen and people bathing in the river don't seem to notice. If they did, they might realize Polyakov was whispering Soviet military secrets.

On the opposite bank, about a quarter of a mile (0.4 km) downstream, stands another fisherman. He hums quietly to himself as he casts his line. Like Polyakov, he seems to be fishing in

the Yamuna River. But this man is actually a US Central Intelligence Agency (CIA) agent.

The two men look like ordinary fishermen, but inside the hollowed-out handles of both their fishing poles are tiny shortwave radios. The metal fishing rods act as the radios' antennae. And when placed in the water, they can pick up acoustic signals. The two fishermen seem like they are talking or humming to themselves, but they are actually passing covert messages back and forth underwater.

THE BIRTH OF A SPY

Polyakov was one of the most important spies during the Cold War. Many historians believe he is responsible for keeping the tension between the US and the USSR, from turning into a full-blown war. With his high Soviet military rank, access to Soviet secrets, and excellent tradecraft skills, Polyakov was nearly a perfect spy.

Polyakov was born in Ukraine in 1921. At the time, Ukraine was a part of the USSR. Polyakov fought for his homeland during World War II. Soon after the war ended in 1945, the USSR's military intelligence agency, known as the GRU, recruited Polyakov. The GRU stationed him in New York City. As far as US officials were concerned, Polyakov was a Soviet officer working at the United Nations. But really, he was directing a secret ring of undercover Soviet spies.

Polyakov had other code names besides "Top Hat." They were "Bourbon," "Donald," and "Roam."

Polyakov received frequent promotions and rose through the GRU ranks. Though he loved his country, Polyakov became disillusioned with the Soviet government sometime between 1959 and 1961. He felt the USSR's Communist government had become corrupt and was making decisions that were not in the best interests of its citizens.

One day Polyakov arranged a secret meeting with officials at the US Federal Bureau of Investigation (FBI) and offered to spy on his home country. He did it because he loved his country and asked for very little in exchange for his information. He believed the information he gave to the FBI and CIA would help the US defeat the corrupt Soviet government.

GENERAL TOP HAT

The CIA gave Polyakov the code name "Top Hat" to protect his identity, and as the Cold War dragged on, he became one of the CIA's most important spies. In 1974, the GRU promoted Polyakov to general, giving him more access to Soviet secrets than ever before.

From his different GRU posts in New York, India, and the USSR, Polyakov provided the US with information on Soviet weapons,

The Minox B was a spy camera used during the Cold War era. Polyakov most likely used this camera or one similar when photographing intelligence for the CIA.

ROBERT HANSSEN

Soviet military intelligence relied on moles for information during the Cold War. One of these was Robert Hanssen. In 1976, Hanssen became an FBI agent. He began spying for the Soviets for money and jewels in 1979. Due to his intelligence training, Hanssen was an extremely effective spy. One of his most damaging acts of espionage was outing Polyakov. His duplicity went undetected for years. But in the late 1990s, the FBI suspected it had a mole. By 2000, it believed it was Hanssen. FBI investigators put surveillance equipment in his office and his assistant provided regular reports on Hanssen's activities. In 2001, investigators finally caught him. During his trial, Hanssen pled guilty to espionage and was sentenced to life in prison.

Hanssen was arrested after leaving a plastic bag filled with classified documents under a footbridge in Foxstone Park, Virginia.

A 2002 FBI review of the FBI security programs called Hanssen's espionage "possibly the worst intelligence disaster in US history."

military strategy, international relations, and espionage techniques. He even shared the names of American spies working for the USSR.

Polyakov took photos of secret GRU documents, hiding the film in hollow rocks for CIA agents to find. With the information Polyakov provided, the CIA was able to understand how the Soviet generals thought and where their priorities lay. This helped US leaders see the Soviets as humans, not just as an enemy.

THE END OF A SPY

In 1980, the GRU called Polyakov back to Moscow, Russia. Polyakov and CIA officials were afraid that he'd been discovered. But Polyakov refused to remain in the US and abandon his country. For a while, everything seemed to be fine. But in 1984, CIA spies found a concerning article in a Soviet sports magazine Polyakov sometimes wrote for. The seemingly innocent article was a recipe for coot, a common waterbird found in Russia. But US officials who worked with Polyakov knew it was a coded message from their spy. And it meant he was in trouble.

Soon after the article was published, Polyakov disappeared. The USSR had arrested him, and in 1988, he was executed for treason. Polyakov had spied for the US for more than 25 years. The covert information he provided helped maintain peace between the US and the Soviets. To some CIA officials, he is considered to be the greatest spy of all time.

Spies working in different countries must come up with cover identities, such as a businessperson or a student, to explain their activities.

CHAPTER 2

ESPIONAGE 101

MANY EXPERTS STILL CONSIDER POLYAKOV TO BE ONE OF the greatest spies to have ever lived. A spy is a person who steals secret information for an intelligence organization. Spies often operate on behalf of a national government or military organization. They usually rely on illegal methods, such as theft and surveillance, to gather their information. This can make a spy's job very dangerous. Spies caught in the act can face arrest, prison, or worse.

SPIES AMONG US

Spies are one of the most important ingredients in human intelligence. Some intelligence is gathered openly through interviews. Other information is collected covertly using spies.

Almost anyone can become a spy. The most important quality for a spy to have is access to secret information. But that doesn't mean a spy needs to be high up in a military, government, or intelligence organization. Spies can be janitors,

US INTELLIGENCE SOURCES

The US government relies on five main methods to gather intelligence. These are sometimes called intelligence collection disciplines. Different government agencies lead each discipline.

OPEN SOURCE

ALL AGENCIES

Gathers information from widely available sources, such as television, radio, newspapers, online articles, research papers, and public records

HUMAN INTELLIGENCE

AGENCIES: FEDERAL BUREAU OF INVESTIGATION (FBI), DOMESTIC INTELLIGENCE; CENTRAL INTELLIGENCE AGENCY (CIA), FOREIGN INTELLIGENCE

Gathers information from human sources

MEASUREMENTS AND SIGNATURES INTELLIGENCE

AGENCY: DEFENSE INTELLIGENCE AGENCY (DIA)

Gathers information from weapons and industrial activities

SIGNALS INTELLIGENCE

AGENCY: NATIONAL SECURITY AGENCY

Gathers information from electronic transmissions, such as phone calls, satellite communications, and online correspondence

IMAGERY INTELLIGENCE

AGENCY: NATIONAL GEOSPATIAL-INTELLIGENCE AGENCY

Gathers information from photos and satellite images

babysitters, friends, or spouses. Anyone in a position to covertly gather intelligence can be a spy.

THE ROAD TO ESPIONAGE

Some spies, such as Polyakov, are trained as intelligence officers. This makes them especially effective. Other spies may receive little to no training. A spy can be a cafeteria worker in a government building with no background in espionage. These spies must rely on their own wits to avoid detection.

People can become spies in many different ways. Some spies are walk-ins, or volunteers, like Polyakov.

Christopher Boyce (*right*) worked with friend and drug dealer Andrew Daulton Lee. Lee helped Boyce deliver intelligence to the Soviet embassy in Mexico.

They are often motivated by patriotism. Like Polyakov, they may feel that their country's government is corrupt.

Other walk-in spies can be motivated by money. In 1974, 21-year-old Christopher Boyce began working as a postal clerk for TRW Systems, a technology company in California that made defense equipment for the US military. Boyce was promoted and

Case officers can use tactics like empathy and having a bond, such as shared interests or friends, to create trust between them and their potential spy.

gained a security clearance. This gave him access to classified CIA satellite technology.

Boyce realized this information could be very valuable. With the help of a friend, Boyce began selling this information to the USSR. The FBI caught the two men 18 months later. They were tried and sentenced to prison.

RECRUITING A SPY

Most spies are recruited. During recruitment, a case officer representing an intelligence organization seeks out an individual they think would make a good spy. They look for people who have access to classified information. But they also must find what might motivate that person to turn against their country. To do this, case officers perform extensive research on the person they are hoping to turn, or make into a spy. This can take months or years.

For example, if a case officer learns their potential spy is having financial problems, they might offer that person money. The case officer might also notice patterns that suggest a promising spy is becoming disillusioned with their own government. Sometimes a case officer finds out their target did something illegal or embarrassing. The officer might use this information to blackmail the person into cooperating.

INTELLIGENCE AND COUNTERINTELLIGENCE

A spy's currency is intelligence. This is any information that could be useful to the organization the spy is working for. During times of war, intelligence might include information about a rival government's military strategy, technology, or weapons.

FBI OR CIA

The two best-known US intelligence agencies are the FBI and the CIA. The FBI was founded in 1908 to combat crime. It gathers intelligence from US citizens and enforces US laws. In 1947, the CIA was founded to gather foreign intelligence. The CIA is not allowed to gather intelligence from US citizens. It also cannot act on any intelligence it receives. Instead, CIA officials must share the information with government leaders or law enforcement agencies.

WHO DO YOU REALLY WORK FOR?

It can be hard to trust where a spy's loyalties truly lie. A spy might pretend to spy for one government while secretly spying for another. Other spies are turned by a rival intelligence organization. These types of spies are known as double agents. Some spies even become triple agents! They work as a spy for one government while pretending to be a double agent for a different government.

In times of peace, intelligence often helps guide a government's foreign policy. This type of intelligence can be used to prevent conflict, such as helping leaders gain insight into a rival government's priorities. Intelligence can also include insight into a rival organization's espionage techniques, including the identities of their spies.

In the world of espionage, counterintelligence is just as important as intelligence. Counterintelligence includes activities designed to mislead the enemy, prevent espionage, and protect national secrets. An intelligence agency might give false information to a spy it knows is working against it.

SPY TALK

The communication between a spy and their handler is essential for a successful espionage operation. The spy might pass secret documents, messages, or other information to their handler. And handlers might send instructions to a spy that could be useful for

THE CHAIN OF INTELLIGENCE

A piece of intelligence gathered by a spy passes through many different hands.

SPY (AGENT, ASSET)

» Collects intelligence

HANDLER (CASE OFFICER, OPERATIONAL OFFICER)

» Recruits and manages the spy

» Plans missions

» Protects the spy's identity

» Collects intelligence from the spy

ANALYST

» Reviews intelligence gathered by spies and other sources

» Determines if the intelligence is reliable

» Consolidates the intelligence into a report

DECISION-MAKER (MILITARY LEADER, LAWMAKER, GOVERNMENT LEADER)

» Reviews the analyst's report

» Decides whether or not to act on the intelligence

their espionage mission. To pass these messages to each other without detection, both the handler and the spy must have good communication methods.

One of the most reliable ways for spy and handler to communicate is through face-to-face meetings. However, this is also one of the riskiest communication techniques. If the spy and handler are noticed together, the spy's identity could be compromised. Instead, spies and handlers mostly rely on covert communication, or COVCOM, techniques to secretly pass information back and forth.

COVCOM

COVCOM can include both low-tech and high-tech methods. Low-tech COVCOM methods use tools such as invisible ink, codes, and ciphers. High-tech COVCOM methods can involve the use of

OFFICE OF TECHNICAL SERVICE

The Office of Technical Service (OTS) is a CIA department dedicated to creating the latest and greatest spy gadgets. Many of these gadgets conceal high-tech espionage devices in everyday objects. A camera might be hidden in a pen. A coat button might contain a secret recording device. And a mobile phone might include lie detection software. To protect its spies, most of the OTS creations are highly classified. Very few people know exactly what the OTS is working on!

Radio receivers could be hidden in modified pipes. The sound waves would travel from the jaw to the ear canal through a person's bones.

special technology to send wireless messages. This technology might be hidden in or disguised as an everyday object, such as a pipe or a clock. Throughout history, spies have found creative and unexpected ways to pass intelligence without getting caught.

TOOLS OF THE TRADE: COVCOM EDITION

Special tools help spies do their work without being detected. Explore some of the most innovative COVCOM techniques used by spies around the world!

ESCAPE MAP CARDS

During World War II, US intelligence agencies hid escape maps inside decks of playing cards. The maps were designed to help US and British prisoners of war trapped in Germany. When one of the cards was soaked in water, it separated into two pieces, revealing a hidden map. It could be combined with other cards' maps to reveal the complete escape route!

US card company Bicycle worked with American and British intelligence agencies to create the escape map card decks. The cards helped at least 32 people escape Colditz Castle in Germany.

DEAD RATS

During the Cold War, CIA officers sometimes hid messages, money, or other secret information inside dead rats and left them at a predetermined location. The rats were covered with hot sauce and special oil to keep other animals from trying to eat them!

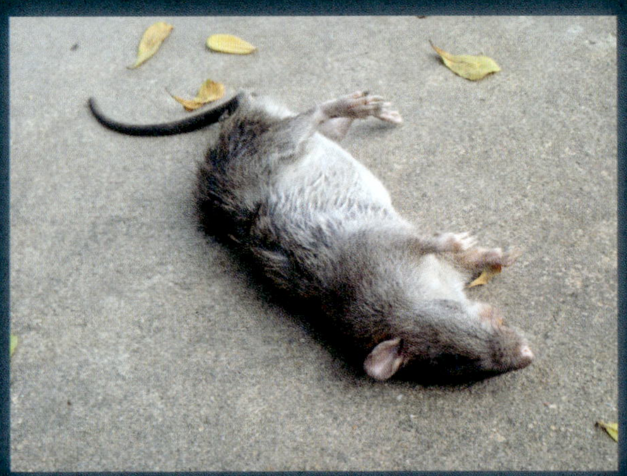

When the CIA creates dead drops, they use objects that blend in with the environment or are so gross that people will not want to touch them.

HOLLOW COINS

Soviet spies have been known to hide secret messages or microdots in fake coins. These coins are hollow inside and have a tiny hole on one side. They can be opened by sticking a needle into the hole.

MICRODOT CAMERA

This tiny camera could take a photo and reduce it to fit on a piece of film no larger than a period. Microdot film produced by the camera could easily be hidden on a letter, object, or piece of clothing.

COMMUNICATIONS ELIMINATOR

In the 1970s, the US military used this device. It was able to block all nearby radio communication. After completing its blocking cycle, the device self-destructed.

SUITCASE TRANSCEIVER

During World War II, British spies used a radio set hidden inside an ordinary-looking suitcase to send and receive secret information.

A hollow silver dollar used by the CIA

Microdot cameras are about the size of a person's thumb. They were popular during the Cold War when transferring intelligence became very difficult.

The Type 3 Mk II, also known as the B2, was a suitcase radio transmitter. It included a receiver, transmitter, power supply, and a box with spare parts and accessories.

November 25, 1783, became known as Evacuation Day. This was the day the British left New York and George Washington and the American troops returned to the city.

CHAPTER 3

EARLY ESPIONAGE

IN LATE 1778, THE AMERICAN REVOLUTION HAD BEEN GOING on for two years. The war seemed to be at a stalemate. France had joined the war as America's ally. But New York City, America's second-largest city, was still under British control.

To win the war, American general George Washington needed vital information on British military operations. He wanted to know what British leaders were planning, such as how many troops they had and their location. At the time, the Americans did not have a reliable intelligence network. But that was about to change. On a cold November day, Washington called Benjamin Tallmadge, a young officer, into his office. He ordered Tallmadge to set up America's first intelligence organization.

As America's first spy handler, Tallmadge recruited a small group of trusted friends to serve as his spies. He assigned each spy a code name to protect their identity. Even Washington didn't know the true identities of Tallmadge's spies. Tallmadge's organization became known as the Culper Spy Ring, based on the code names of two of its members, Abraham Woodhull AKA Samuel Culper, and Robert Townsend AKA Culper Jr. The Culper Spy ring soon developed clever COVCOM methods to securely exchange information.

CLOTHES, CIPHERS, AND INVISIBLE INK

The Culper Spy Ring found most of its information at a Long Island restaurant and store owned by Townsend. These places were popular gathering spots for many British soldiers. There, the spies acquired information on British troop numbers and movements, supplies, ship movements, and more.

Washington gave Benjamin Tallmadge the title and position of director of military intelligence. When the war ended, Tallmadge was elected to the US House of Representatives.

A courier then transported messages with this information to and from Washington. To protect the ring, Tallmadge's spies used different COVCOM techniques. All messages were written using a complex numerical cipher system, which could only be decrypted using a key known as the Culper Code Book.

Washington also demanded that all messages be written in invisible ink. This ink was a mixture of water and a chemical compound called ferrous sulfate. The message could only be revealed when exposed to heat from a flame, such as a candle, or a chemical compound called sodium carbonate. The spies also wrote

CODE OR CIPHER?

Codes and ciphers are messages that are changed to hide their true meaning. In a code, words are replaced with other numbers or words. For example, the word *pickle* might be code for "A dead drop is ready." A cipher uses an algorithm to change all the elements of a message into different characters. For example, the letter e might be represented by the numeral 3. Ciphers often look like a random string of letters, numbers, and symbols. To make a cipher even more complicated, the message contents might be rearranged!

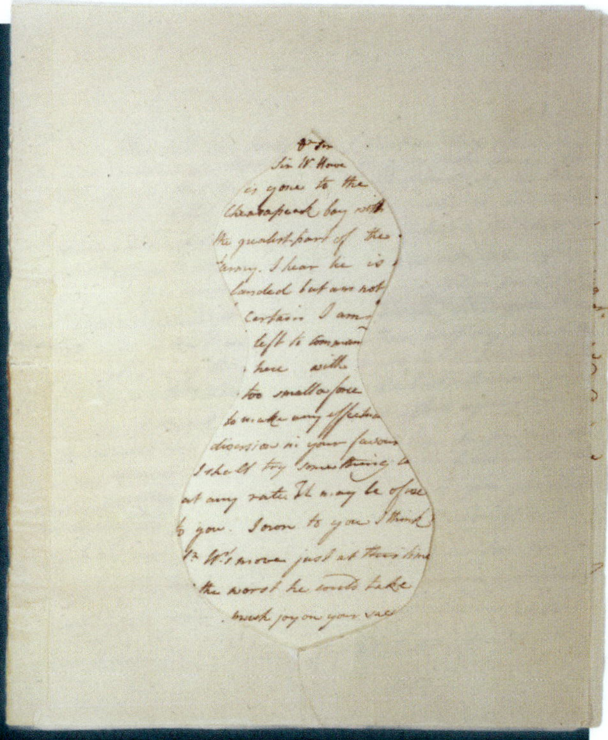

During the American Revolution, the British used masked letters to send coded messages. This involved writing a letter where the hidden message could only be read using a mask cutout.

some of their invisible messages in printed pamphlets or books, which were less suspicious to British agents than personal letters. Some messages were also hidden in hollowed-out quills, buttons, or musket balls. The arrangement of clothes on a clothesline signaled that a message was ready for the courier and where it was hidden. These techniques later became known as dead drops.

Culper spies informed Washington of British movements in and around New York City. The spies' work also revealed the identities

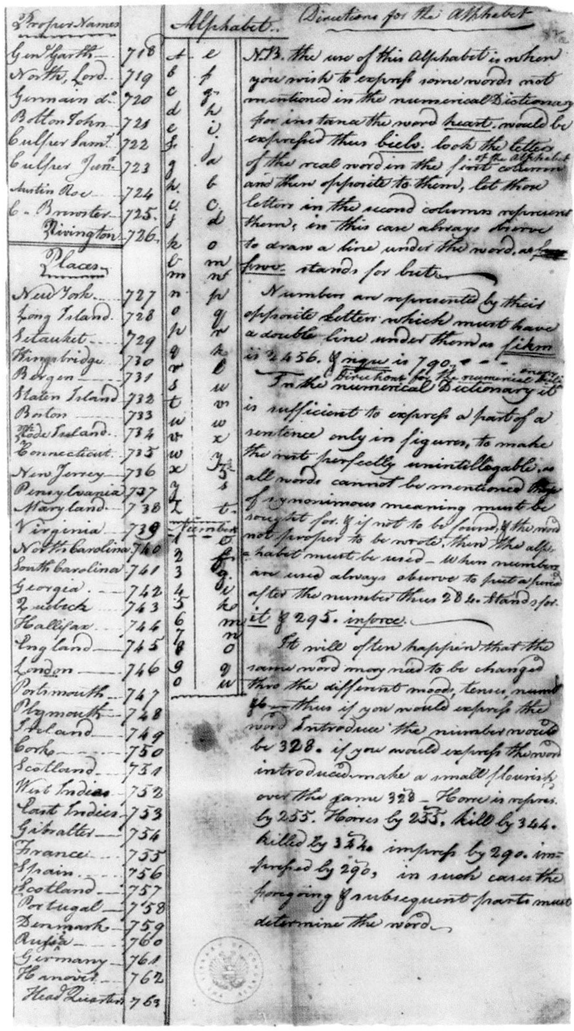

The Culper Code Book helped
protect the communications and
identities of the Culper Spy Ring.
The book included 763 numbers,
each matching a different word.

of British spies, including British spymaster John André. In 1780, Culper spies passed their most important message to Washington. British General Henry Clinton was preparing troops for an attack on Rhode Island. Washington quickly positioned his army to protect the colony and the French ships docked there. This led to Clinton canceling his attack.

Thanks to their COVCOM methods, no member of the Culper Spy Ring was ever caught. This was largely because they combined their espionage operations with everyday activities, such as laundry and shopping, making them harder to detect. Many historians believe America's espionage operations were crucial to their military success in the Revolutionary War. On September 3, 1783, British and American leaders signed the Treaty of Paris, officially ending the war. The US had won. According to British intelligence officer George Beckwith, "Washington did not really outfight the British. He simply out-spied us."

BENEDICT ARNOLD

One of the most infamous spies of the Revolutionary War was Benedict Arnold, a once-promising American general. Arnold was born in Connecticut in 1741. In 1775, he volunteered for the newly formed American military. After a series of military successes, Arnold was promoted to general. In 1777, Congress denied Arnold another promotion. In 1778, Arnold was put in command of Philadelphia. There, he began spending time with British supporters, known as Loyalists. Arnold married Loyalist Peggy Shippen in 1779, and she introduced him to British spymaster John André. Arnold agreed to serve as one of André's spies. He passed secret documents to André, including maps of West Point, an important American fort. In 1780, thanks to the Culper spies, André was captured and Arnold's duplicity was revealed. André was executed, but Arnold escaped to Great Britain.

Benedict Arnold felt that he did not receive enough recognition for his accomplishments in the Continental Army. So he agreed to spy for the British for money.

General Ulysses S. Grant
went on to become the
commanding general of the
Union Army and, later,
president of the US.

CHAPTER 4

CHANGING TECHNOLOGY

IN 1862, THE AMERICAN CIVIL WAR HAD BEEN RAGING ON for one year. The North, or the Union, was fighting against the South, or the Confederacy. Union general Henry Halleck was having trouble trying to reach General Ulysses S. Grant, who was leading Union troops in Tennessee.

Halleck was based in St. Louis, Missouri, and used a revolutionary new technology called the telegraph to send messages to Grant. In the past, a courier delivered all wartime messages. But the telegraph was able to send messages from Missouri to Tennessee and back in a matter of seconds. Using the telegraph, Halleck ordered Grant to send him updates on his progress and troop movements. But Grant remained silent.

Finally, Halleck became so fed up, he recommended that Grant be removed from duty. Halleck launched an investigation into Grant's insubordination. But the investigation revealed that a telegraph operator in Cairo, Illinois, was a Confederate spy. The spy had intercepted Halleck's messages and delivered them to Confederate leaders instead of sending them to Grant in Tennessee. Grant's name was cleared!

LINCOLN'S LINE

The telegraph was a vital communication device during the Civil War, particularly for the Union. US president and Union commander Abraham Lincoln used the telegraph to communicate with his generals. He sent telegraph messages to media outlets, such as newspapers, hoping to control the war narrative. Lincoln relied on the technology so much, he sometimes slept in the telegraph operator's office.

Lincoln also used the telegraph to spy on Americans. All telegraph messages were routed through Secretary of War Edwin Stanton's office before being sent on. Some of these messages never arrived to their intended recipients. This form of espionage

Stanton worked to push a bill through Congress that gave the government control of the telegraph. This gave Stanton the ability to control all the telegraph communications in the US.

allowed Union leaders to understand what people were thinking and feeling about the war. Union leaders even controlled what was being said about the war by arresting journalists who were revealed to be pro-Confederacy through their telegraph messages.

GEORGE "LIGHTNING" ELLSWORTH

The Confederacy had fewer telegraph lines than the Union, but it used the technology to further its cause. George "Lightning" Ellsworth was one of the most famous spies of the Civil War. And his tool of choice was the telegraph.

THE TERRIFIC TELEGRAPH

American painter Samuel F.B. Morse invented the telegraph in 1837. Morse developed a code based on a system of dots and dashes that represented letters and numbers. A transmitter sent the dots and dashes, in the form of long and short electric pulses, through a wire from one telegraph station to a receiver at another station. There, the message could be decoded by the telegraph operator. By 1861, telegraph wires stretched across the US, making instant long-distance communication possible.

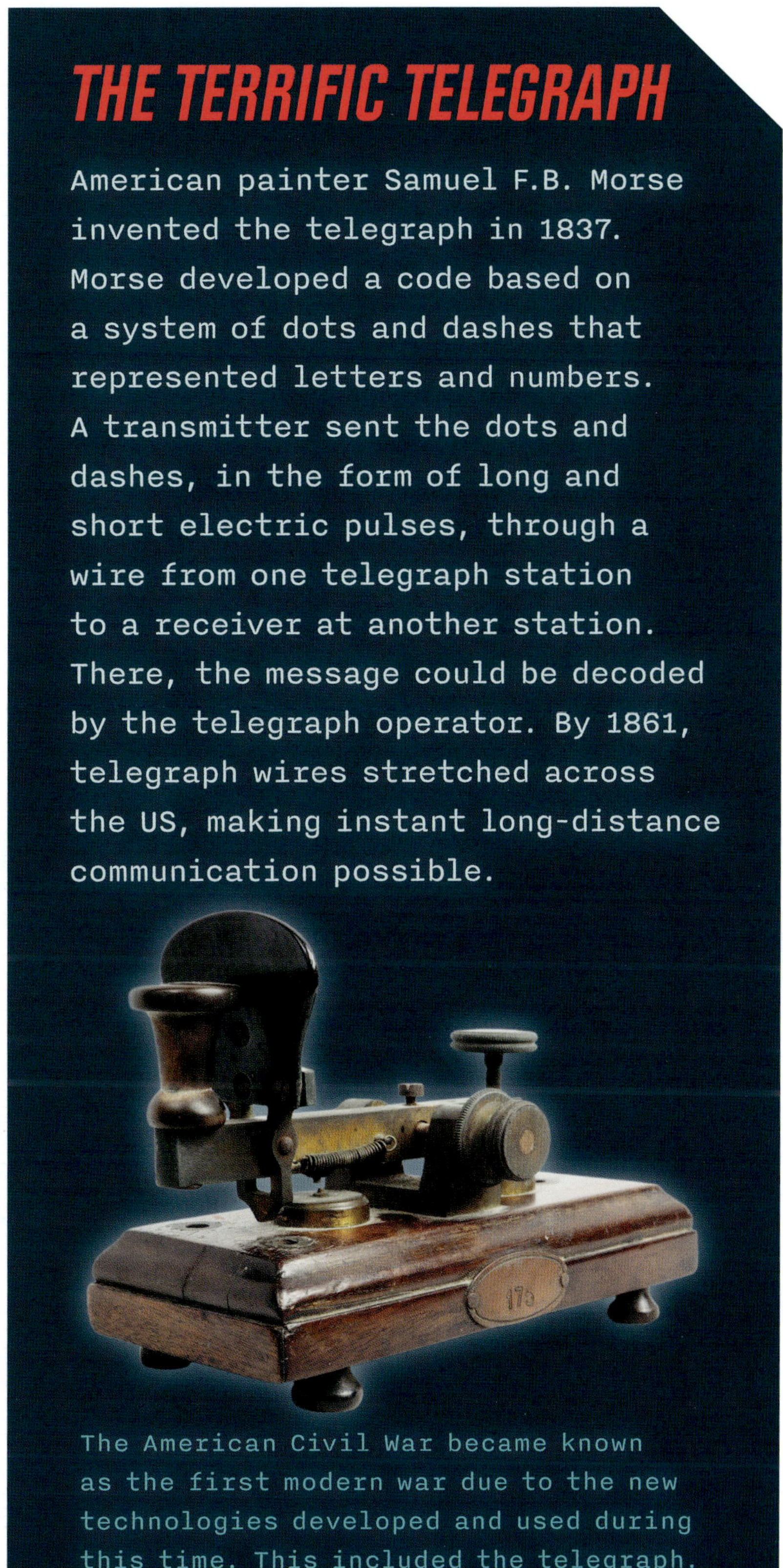

The American Civil War became known as the first modern war due to the new technologies developed and used during this time. This included the telegraph.

Ellsworth worked for Confederate general John Hunt Morgan, who was stationed in Kentucky. Ellsworth had a special pocket-sized tool he could attach to telegraph wires. The instrument detected the electrical pulses through the wire, allowing him to listen to

messages before they reached the Union telegraph station. This process became known as tapping the wire. Ellsworth also used his tool to send messages containing false information to the Union operator. He was especially skilled at mimicking the writing styles of the telegrams he listened to, making his false messages more convincing.

Ellsworth occasionally revealed himself by sending playful messages to Union leaders. He sent one message to Union general Jeremiah Boyle on behalf of Morgan that said, "Good morning, Jerry. This telegraph is a neat institution. You should destroy it as it keeps me posted too well. My friend Ellsworth has all your dispatches since July 10 on file. Do you wish copies?" Ellsworth's espionage techniques were so successful that both Confederate and Union leaders copied them. By the end of the war, both sides frequently tapped telegraph wires to spy on their enemy and spread false information. After the Civil War ended in 1865, the technology continued to advance in ways that would transform espionage in the years to come.

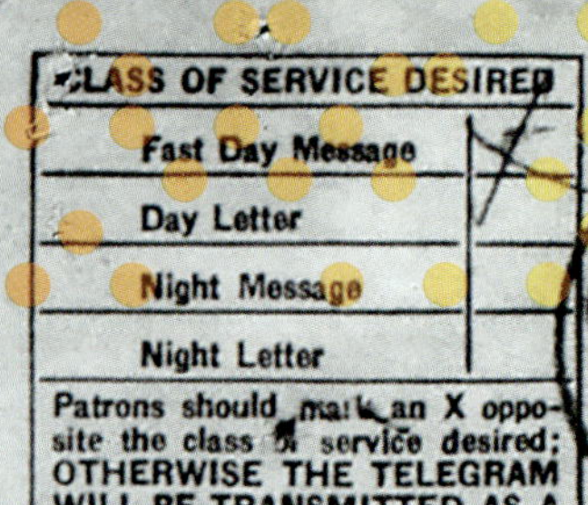

On March 1, 1917, the American press published the Zimmermann Telegram. About a month later, the US declared war on Germany and the Central Powers.

Send the following telegram, subject to on back hereof, which are hereby ag   via Galveston

GERMAN LEGATION

MEXICO CITY

130	13042	13401	8501	115	3528	416	17214	6
18147	18222	21560	10247	11518	23677	13605	3	
98092	5905	11311	10392	10371	0302	21290	5161	
23571	17504	11269	18276	18101	0317	0228	1769	
23284	22200	19452	21589	67893	5569	13918	895	
1333	4725	4458	5905	17166	13851	4458	17149	
13850	12224	6929	14991	7382	15857	67893	1421	
5870	17553	67893	5870	5454	16102	15217	22801	
21001	17388	7446	23638	18222	6719	14331	150	
3156	23552	22096	21604	4797	9497	22464	2085	
23610	18140	22260	5905	13347	20420	39689	1373	
6929	5275	18507	52262	1340	22049	13339	11265	
10439	14814	4178	6992	8784	7632	7357	6926	
21100	21272	9346	9559	22464	15874	18502	1850	
2188	5376	7381	98092	16127	13486	9350	9220	
5144	2831	17920	11347	17142	11264	7667	7762	
10482	97556	3569	3670					

BERNSTORFF.

CHAPTER 5

THE WORLD AT WAR

IN THE WINTER OF 1917, ROOM 40 OF LONDON, ENGLAND'S OLD Admiralty Building was a busy place. The room, which contained an entire department, was filled with the clicking of keys and the scratching of pencils on paper. World War I had been ongoing since 1914, and the Allies needed all the help they could get to defeat their German enemy.

The Germans often communicated using coded messages sent through encrypted radio transmissions. British leaders had set up a code-breaking center to intercept and decode these messages. In doing so, they hoped to learn as much about their enemy as possible. Hundreds of British radio operators and cryptographers worked night and day to intercept and decode German messages.

On January 16, the British received the message they needed. Cryptographers in Room 40 intercepted and decoded a cipher from German foreign secretary Arthur Zimmermann intended for leaders in Mexico. The telegram proposed that Mexico join with Germany to try to capture territory in the American Southwest.

Up to this point, US president Woodrow Wilson had refused to involve the US and its powerful military in the war. But that changed when British officials shared the decoded message, known as the Zimmermann Telegram, with US leaders. Soon after, the US officially entered World War I and helped lead the Allies to victory.

British codebreakers deciphered more than 15,000 messages during World War I while working in the Old Admiralty Building (*pictured*).

LOW-TECH COVCOM

Not all World War I communication used wireless technology. British spies sometimes communicated with their handlers using coded messages attached to pigeons or dogs.

THE RISE OF RADIO

In 1894, Italian inventor Guglielmo Marconi started developing a wireless communication system that could send messages using a type of electromagnetic radiation known as radio waves. These waves of energy carried electronic signals through the air. Marconi also built a device that used these radio waves to send messages wirelessly.

Experts consider Guglielmo Marconi to be the inventor of radio due to his wireless telegraph system.

Thanks to Marconi, military leaders no longer needed a wired telegraph station to send messages back and forth. All they needed was a wireless receiver and transmitter. During World War I, the German Navy relied on wireless technology to communicate with leaders in Germany while at sea.

The trouble with wireless communication was that anyone with a receiver could easily intercept it. That meant all messages had to be encrypted. Cryptographers on each side developed increasingly complex codes and ciphers to protect their information. So, many intercepted messages sounded like nonsense at first. Cryptographers may have used words like *bacon* to refer to weapons or *cabin* to refer to cars. Meanwhile, spies and codebreakers worked to decode their enemy's messages and discover their secrets.

UNBREAKABLE CODES

Codes had been a crucial part of COVCOM for centuries, but up until World War I, all codes and ciphers were created by humans. This meant they could all theoretically be broken by humans. That changed in 1917, when inventor Edward Hebern created the first electronic cipher machine called the Hebern Rotor Machine.

Hebern's device featured a typewriter with an electric rotor that scrambled letters as they were typed. To decode the message, the

After creating the Hebern Rotor Machine (*pictured*), Hebern later made three-rotor and five-rotor versions. These made the ciphers stronger while still being easy to use.

recipient inserted the same rotor on their machine in the opposite direction and retyped the encoded message. Though Hebern's machine was the first of its kind, its ciphers were relatively simple, so it never gained widespread use. But a similar machine, created just a few years later, would change the course of the next major war, World War II.

CRACKING ENIGMA

Throughout World War II, the Germans used a machine called Enigma to encrypt messages for radio transmission. The machine worked like the Hebern Rotor Machine, but with many more letter combinations. To make it even more secure, Enigma's settings were recalibrated daily. This meant an entirely new code was created every day.

Enigma provided billions of ways for Germans to encode their messages, making the code nearly impossible to crack. Polish mathematicians managed to break the code early in the war. But

German cryptographers continued to change and improve Enigma, once again making its codes unbreakable.

In 1939, British mathematician Alan Turing was charged with breaking Enigma once and for all. Turing designed his own machine, called Bombe, which helped decrypt Enigma's coded messages. Turing and other codebreakers found words that were more likely to appear in messages, such as the German words for *weather*, *the*, or *Hitler*, the name of Germany's leader. Using these words and

NAVAJO CODE TALKERS

In 1942, the US military recruited 29 Navajo men to create an unbreakable code based on the Navajo language. The language, which had no written form at the time, was extraordinarily complex, making it challenging for non-Navajo speakers to learn. The Navajo men, known as the Navajo Code Talkers, substituted Navajo words for key military words and phrases, creating a quick and highly accurate code. This helped the US and its allies win important battles.

Private First Class Preston Toledo (*left*) and Private First Class Frank Toledo were Navajo Code Talkers. They used a field radio to transmit their messages.

the Bombe machine, Turing and his
fellow codebreakers were able to
figure out the settings for Enigma
each day, cracking the code!

MICRODOTS AND EXPLODING NOTEBOOKS

Codes and ciphers were an
important part of World War II
COVCOM. But they were not the
only communication methods
used by military and intelligence
organizations. These organizations
also used other COVCOM tools to
communicate with their spies.

Microdots were an invention
that had been around since the
1870s. These became a favored
communication technique used by
spies during World War II.

Microdots are created by
reducing information, such as text or
an image, to an almost unimaginably
small size. A microdot can be smaller than a period in a book! A
spy would first photograph secret materials. They would then use
a series of lenses to copy and reduce the size of the photo until it
was a tiny dot. The image could then be printed on a special type of
photographic film and attached to almost any object, including toys

The German Enigma machine
(*pictured*) was similar to
the Hebern Rotor Machine.
Both machines used an
electromechanical rotor
mechanism to scramble the
typed letters.

JOSEPHINE BAKER

World War II provided many opportunities for spies to shine. But most spies tried to avoid the spotlight. American dancer, singer, and actress Josephine Baker was one of the most famous entertainers of her time. But she had a secret identity during World War II. She was a spy for the Allies. During the war, Baker performed in Paris, France. German officers frequently attended her performances and Baker was able to eavesdrop on their conversations, gathering important military intelligence. She passed these secrets to Allied officials by writing messages on sheet music using invisible ink!

Josephine Baker also worked in North Africa during World War II. She would gather information and pin the intelligence to the inside of her underwear to avoid detection.

and clothing. Some microdots were attached to letters and left in dead drop locations.

Pyrofilm combustible notebooks were another method spies used to pass sensitive information during World War II. These looked like regular notebooks, but they contained a special kind of flammable film, called pyrofilm, and included a special pencil. When the eraser was pulled out of the pencil near the notebook, the entire notebook would burst into flames, destroying any secret messages written within.

The espionage techniques developed during World Wars I and II would soon come in handy. The US was about to enter a conflict built around espionage. The Cold War was about to begin.

Spies can use almost any object to hide microdots. A German spy hid microdots on a doll when smuggling intelligence into Germany.

Ames used a mailbox on the corner of
37th and R Streets as a dead drop.
He made a chalk mark above the postal
seal to signal his Soviet handlers.

CHAPTER 6

COLD WAR ESPIONAGE

ALDRICH AMES SEEMED LIKE THE PERFECT CIA AGENT. AS THE son of a CIA analyst, Ames was familiar with how the organization worked. After completing the CIA Career Trainee Program, Ames recruited Soviet spies for the US and unmasked enemy spies. But his experience also made him perfect for another role, a double agent.

In 1985, Ames agreed to sell US intelligence to the USSR. He gave them the names of US agents working in the USSR and insight into how the CIA operated.

To communicate with his USSR handlers, Ames made a small chalk mark on a mailbox near his home in Washington, DC. The mark was barely noticeable to the average passerby. But it told Ames's Soviet connection that intelligence was ready for pickup and where to find it. Ames hid intelligence in many different locations throughout the Washington, DC, area.

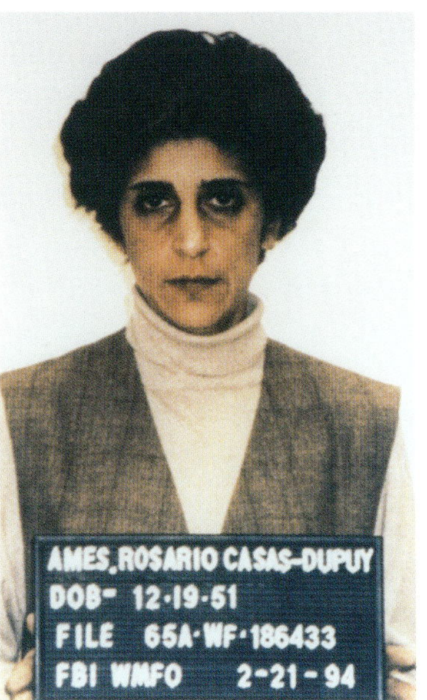

Aldrich Ames and his wife received more than $2.7 million for spying. This is the largest amount of money the USSR ever paid an American spy.

A couple of his hiding spots included a park drainpipe and underneath a small bridge. After collecting the intelligence, Ames's handler would leave money and additional instructions for Ames. The FBI finally caught and arrested Ames in 1994. He pled guilty during his trial and was sentenced to prison.

The Cold War was a time of great mistrust. Spies seemed to be everywhere. Both US and Soviet intelligence organizations were constantly trying

The CIA and British Secret Intelligence Service built a tunnel under Berlin where they hid equipment used to tap German phone lines.

to unmask the spies working against them. Face-to-face meetings were more dangerous than ever. So spies and their handlers resorted to less noticeable methods of communication.

DEAD DROPS

Dead drops, like the ones Ames and his handler used, were one of the most tried-and-true Cold War communication methods. In a dead drop, the spy or handler leaves a message, money, or electronic device in an agreed-upon location for the other party to retrieve later. This location might be a hollow rock, behind a loose brick, or under a hotel dresser. In 2021, a US Navy nuclear engineer was arrested for hiding a memory card in a half-eaten sandwich and leaving it in a dead drop location. A signal between the spy and handler indicated that a dead drop was ready. This signal had to be almost unnoticeable. It might be a lipstick

USSR INTELLIGENCE ORGANIZATIONS

During the Cold War, the USSR had two main intelligence organizations, the KGB and the GRU. The KGB was the intelligence organization for the USSR's Communist Party. It gathered foreign intelligence, often through espionage. During the Cold War, the group also acted as a secret police force. The KGB ended with the collapse of the USSR in 1991. The GRU is the highly secretive foreign intelligence organization for the Russian military. Like the KGB, it uses spies, but less is known about its operations. And unlike the KGB, the GRU is still in operation.

WRITING AN UNBREAKABLE CODE

During the Cold War, the USSR used a highly complex code system. The message writer used a code book to choose a group of four-digit numbers called a code group. Each code group represented a letter or word. Then the four-digit code group numbers were converted to five-digit numbers. These numbers were encrypted again, using a second set of numbers called a key. The keys were completely random and never reused.

Any object could be turned into a dead drop. Dead drop spikes were used to hide intelligence. They could be pushed into the ground, making them undetectable.

mark on a signpost or piece of string tied around a telephone pole.

PROJECT VENONA

Cold War espionage also relied on intercepting and decoding Soviet messages. In 1943, US intelligence agencies set up a secret program code-named VENONA to aid in this mission. At the time, the US was able to intercept KGB messages. But the messages were written in what seemed to be an unbreakable code. Agents had no means of reading the valuable intelligence in the messages. This was where project VENONA came in.

VENONA employed some of the best codebreakers in the US. Ninety percent

Meredith Gardner (*left*) was credited for breaking the Soviet cipher, but much of the groundwork behind his success was done by women.

of VENONA's codebreakers were women who used to be schoolteachers, and many were new to cryptography. But they all had a rare talent for numbers.

In 1946, VENONA codebreakers managed to crack the Soviets' "unbreakable code." For the next 34 years, the project worked to decode Soviet messages. VENONA's codebreakers decoded more than 3,000 messages, revealing the identities of many Soviet spies along with other crucial information.

The Cold War may have ended in 1991, but espionage activities between Russia and the US continued. With new technology came new and improved communication techniques. And with the rise of the internet in the early 2000s, spy communication became harder to detect than ever before.

Cuba recruited Montes because she disagreed with US foreign policy. While working at the DIA headquarters (*pictured*), security knew about her views but didn't think she was a spy.

CHAPTER 7

SPYING INTO THE FUTURE

In 2001, FBI agents stormed the Washington, DC, home of Ana Montes. Montes had been serving as a Cuban analyst for the US Defense Intelligence Agency (DIA) since 1985. She excelled at her job and became one of the DIA's best and most trusted analysts. But due to the suspicions of one of her colleagues, the FBI opened an investigation on Montes in 2000. While raiding her home, FBI agents found a laptop containing decades of secret information under Montes's bed. One of the DIA's top analysts was a spy.

Montes was able to avoid capture for years because of her amazing memory. Instead of photographing or stealing sensitive documents, Montes memorized details of them while at work. Each evening when she got home, Montes typed the intelligence onto her laptop. After encrypting her message, she passed it to her Cuban

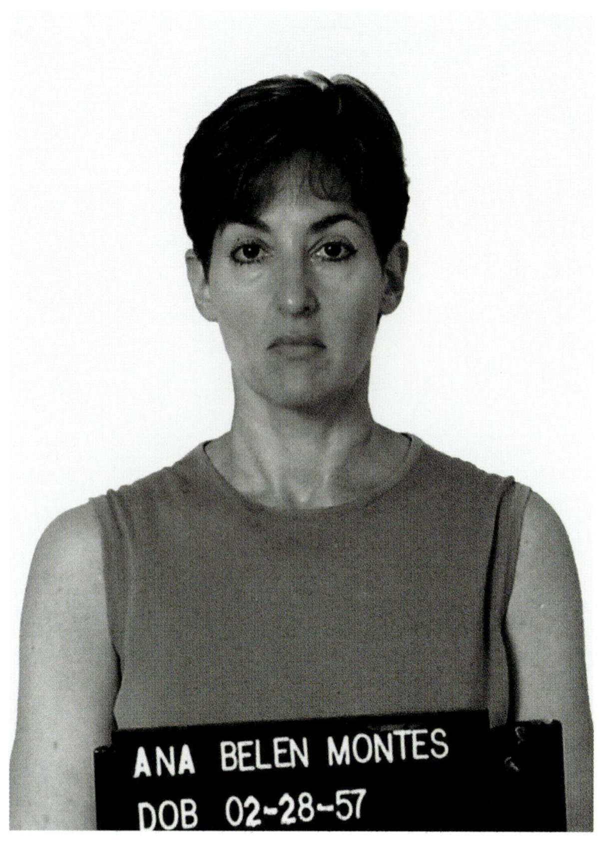

After Montes was released from prison on January 6, 2023, she moved back to her home in Puerto Rico.

handler, sometimes at a busy restaurant or by traveling to Cuba under a false identity.

Despite the technology available, Montes often used low-tech COVCOM techniques. Montes's handlers sent her instructions using coded radio messages. She wrote them down on water-soluble paper which instantly dissolved when wet. Montes also communicated with her handlers using coded numerical messages left near

DNA MESSAGES

In 1999, researchers created a method to conceal secret messages in human DNA. They developed a 3-letter code, then encoded the key into a strand of human DNA. To access the key, the recipient must isolate that specific DNA strand. It is not known if intelligence agencies decided to use this technique after its creation.

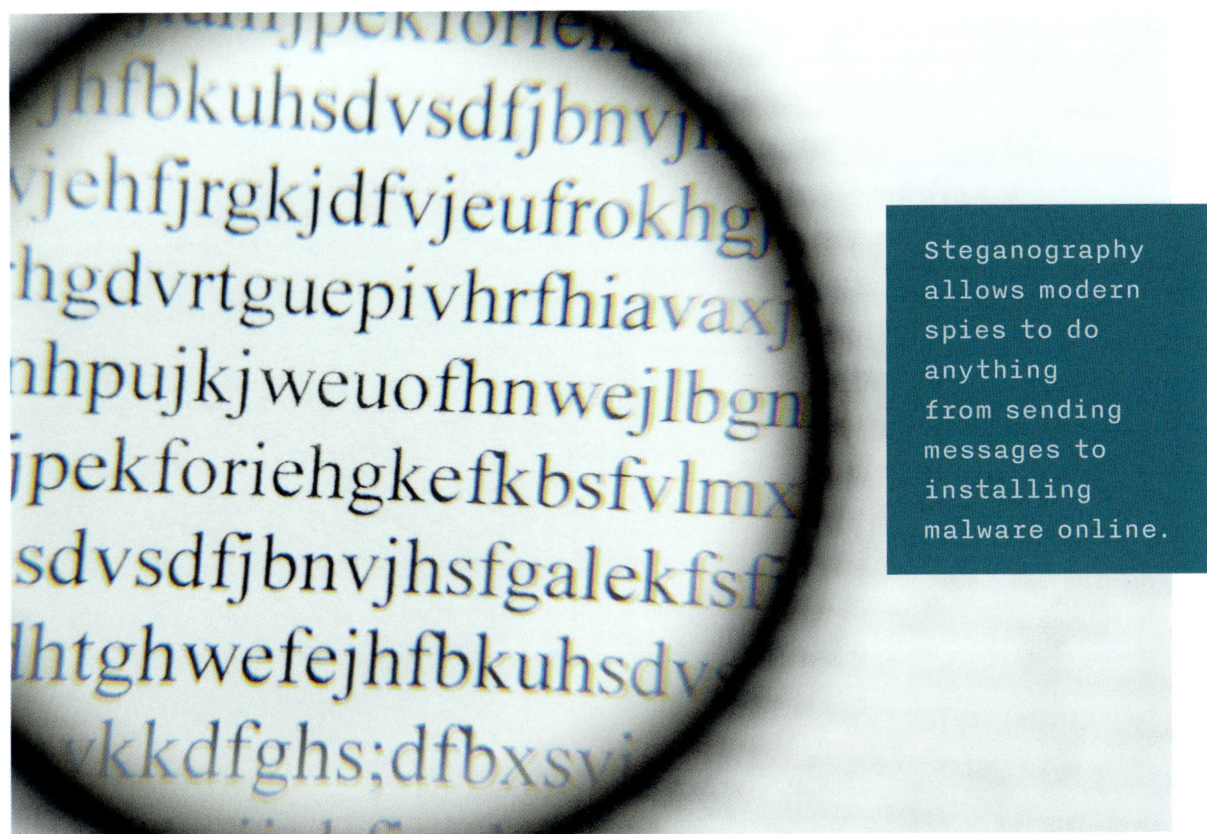

public telephones. Still, as technology changes, modern spies have more communication options to choose from than ever before.

STEGANOGRAPHY

Steganography is a COVCOM technique that involves hiding secret messages in another message, image, or object. Steganography has been used for thousands of years, with secret messages woven into sweaters or even hidden in tattoos. Microdots have been a tried-and-true steganography method since World War II. But the rise of digital information has made steganography more popular than ever.

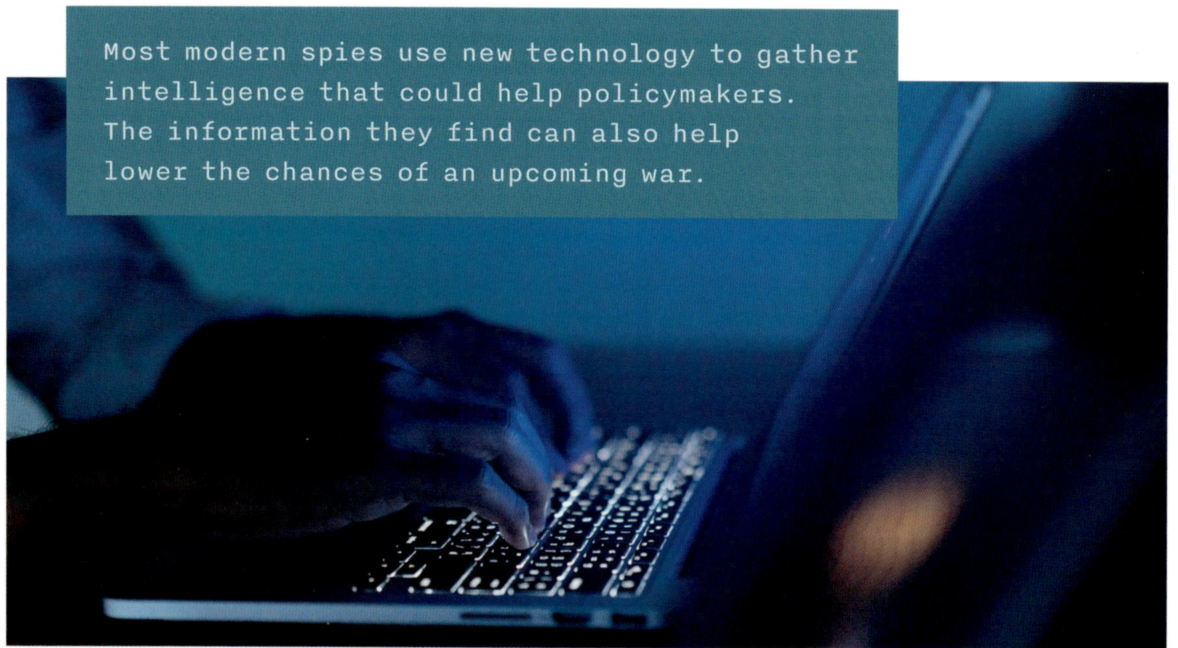

CORPORATE ESPIONAGE

Not all spies work on behalf of government intelligence
agencies. Corporations may occasionally hire
individuals to spy on their behalf. Corporate spies
work to steal secret information from a company's
competitor. In 2006, Joya Williams, a secretary for
the soft drink company Coca-Cola, was arrested for
attempting to sell company secrets to Coca-Cola's
biggest competitor, Pepsi.

Modern spies can hide information in the code of any online
file, from pictures to videos to news articles. With the rise of social
media and digital gaming, there is more online content than ever
before, creating plenty of places for a spy to hide a secret message.

BECOMING AN AGENT

Getting a job at the CIA or FBI is a sure way to find yourself on the front lines of covert intelligence. To become a CIA or FBI agent, you must be a US citizen with a college degree. It also helps to speak more than one language. Aspiring agents need to complete a lengthy application process and pass a background check. They also need to pass medical and fitness requirements before beginning a rigorous training program.

SPIES TODAY

The high-stakes espionage of the World Wars and the Cold War may be in the past. New technology such as artificial intelligence, drones, and online data can do some of the same intelligence sourcing done by human agents. But spies haven't faded into the background. The US is believed to have more than 10,000 spies scattered around the world, feeding information to intelligence agencies.

Modern spies continue to provide intelligence on other governments. But these spies may also infiltrate terrorist organizations and crime rings. Modern spies can also be used to target private companies, especially tech and finance companies.

Being a spy is a dangerous job. They are unlikely to receive any credit for their work. And most spies disappear into history when their careers are over.

SO YOU WANT TO BE A SPY?

Spies can be anywhere and everywhere. Your soccer coach, your bus driver, or even your mom could be a spy! But being a spy who can maintain cover while providing intelligence takes a special set of skills. Do you have what it takes to master the art of COVCOM? Complete the missions below to find out!

MISSION 1
DIY INVISIBLE INK

WHAT YOU NEED

2 small cups
1 cup water
1 tablespoon
  baking soda

spoon
writing tool:
  calligraphy pen or
  small paintbrushes

paper
large paintbrush
½ cup rubbing alcohol
1 teaspoon turmeric

STEPS

1. In a small cup, mix water and baking soda together. This is the invisible ink!

2. Write a secret message on the paper using a writing tool and the invisible ink. Allow it to dry completely.

3. In another small cup, mix rubbing alcohol and turmeric together. This is the revealer!

4. Once your message is dry, paint over it with the revealer. Now wait for the secret message to appear!

CRACK THE CODE

Can you use the key to solve the cipher below?

—George Herbert, English poet circa 1630

CIPHER KEY

a =	b =	c =	d =	e =	f =	g =	h =	i =
j =	k =	l =	m =	n =	o =	p =	q =	r =
s =	t =	u =	v =	w =	x =	y =	z =	

Cipher solution: The life of spies is to know, not to be known.

MISSION 3
DESIGN A DEAD DROP

WHAT YOU NEED

small container
camouflage items

hot glue gun
secret message or map

STEPS

1. Find the best place for your dead drop. It can be outside in nature or hidden in your home.

2. Gather camouflage materials and glue them to the container, covering as much of the surface as you can.

3. Create your secret message or map and place it in the container. This is your dead drop.

4. Hide your dead drop for another agent to pick up.

TIMELINE

The American Revolutionary War
1775–1783

American general Benedict Arnold begins spying for the British.
1779

The American Civil War
1861–1865

World War I
1914–1918

British cryptographers intercept and decode the Zimmermann Telegram.
1917

1778
American general George Washington orders Benjamin Tallmadge to form an intelligence organization that becomes known as the Culper Spy Ring.

1894
Guglielmo Marconi invents radio communication.

1939–1945
World War II

1941
Alan Turing cracks the German Enigma machine.

The Navajo Code Talkers begin encoding intelligence for the US military.

1942

GRU officer Dmitri Polyakov begins spying for the US.

CIRCA 1960

CIA agent Aldrich Ames is arrested for selling US intelligence to the USSR.

1994

1946
VENONA codebreakers crack the Soviets' code.

1947–1991
The Cold War

1979
FBI agent Robert Hanssen begins spying for the USSR.

2001
FBI agents arrest longtime DIA analyst Ana Montes for spying for Cuba.

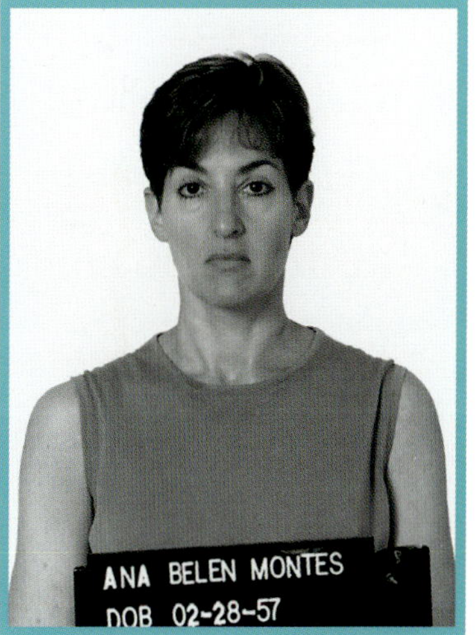

GLOSSARY

algorithm—a set of steps that are followed in order to solve a mathematical problem or to complete a computer process.

classified—kept from the public in order to protect national security.

Cold War—a period of tension and hostility between the US and its allies and the USSR and its allies after World War II.

courier—a messenger, especially in secretive, military, or diplomatic roles.

COVCOM—covert communication. Covert communication is the secret exchange of information or data.

cryptography—the coding and decoding of secret messages. A cryptographer is a person who codes and decodes secret messages.

decrypt—to change from a set of letters, numbers, or symbols that cannot be understood into words that can be understood.

duplicity—speaking or acting in two different ways in order to deceive.

eavesdrop—to secretly listen to a private conversation.

encrypt—to convert information or data into a cipher or code to prevent unauthorized access.

espionage—the secret gathering of information on others.

foreign policy—a sovereign state's approach to interacting with other sovereign states.

infiltrate—to enter a place secretly and without permission.

insubordination—refusal to obey a superior.

intercept—to interrupt something on its way from one place to another.

mole—a spy who establishes a long-term cover within an organization.

patriotism—love of and devotion to one's country.

potential—having the ability to occur or be achieved in the future.

recalibrate—to calibrate is to adjust precisely for a particular function. To recalibrate is to calibrate something again.

shortwave—a radio wave that has a wavelength between 10 and 100 meters.

stalemate—a contest or battle in which neither side can gain an advantage or win.

surveillance—close observation of someone or something.

tradecraft—the methods developed by intelligence operatives to conduct their operations.

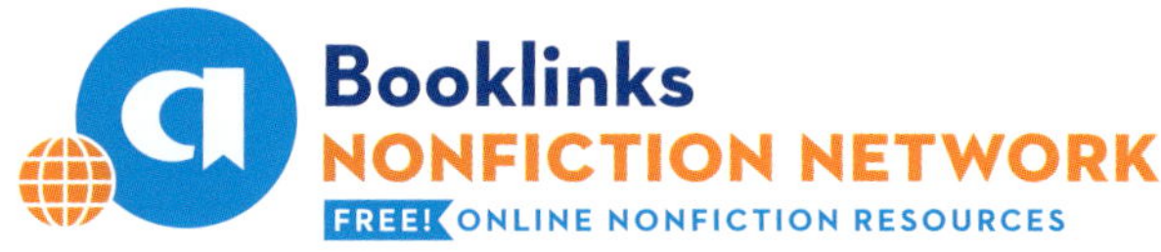

To learn more about spy communication, please visit **abdobooklinks.com** or scan this QR code. These links are routinely monitored and updated to provide the most current information available.

INDEX